Endorsements for the Church Questions Series

"Christians are pressed by very real questions. How does Scripture structure a church, order worship, organize ministry, and define biblical leadership? Those are just examples of the questions that are answered clearly, carefully, and winsomely in this new series from 9Marks. I am so thankful for this ministry and for its incredibly healthy and hopeful influence in so many faithful churches. I eagerly commend this series."

R. Albert Mohler Jr., President, The Southern Baptist Theological Seminary

"Sincere questions deserve thoughtful answers. If you're not sure where to start in answering these questions, let this series serve as a diving board into the pool. These minibooks are winsomely to-the-point and great to read together with one friend or one hundred friends."

Gloria Furman, author, *Missional Motherhood* and *The Pastor's Wife*

T0326851

"As a pastor, I get asked lots of questions. I'm approached by unbelievers seeking to understand the gospel, new believers unsure about next steps, and maturing believers wanting help answering questions from their Christian family, friends, neighbors, or coworkers. It's in these moments that I wish I had a book to give them that was brief, answered their questions, and pointed them in the right direction for further study. Church Questions is a series that provides just that. Each booklet tackles one question in a biblical, brief, and practical manner. The series may be called Church Questions, but it could be called 'Church Answers.' I intend to pick these up by the dozens and give them away regularly. You should too."

Juan R. Sanchez, Senior Pastor, High Pointe Baptist Church, Austin, Texas

"Where can we Christians find reliable answers to our common questions about life together at church—without having to plow through long, expensive books? The Church Questions booklets meet our need with answers that are biblical, thoughtful, and practical. For pastors, this series will prove a trustworthy resource for guiding church members toward deeper wisdom and stronger unity."

Ray Ortlund, President, Renewal Ministries

What If I've Been Hurt by My Church?

Church Questions

What If I've Been Hurt by My Church?

Daniel P. Miller

:: CROSSWAY®

WHEATON, ILLINOIS

What If I've been Hurt by My Church?

© 2024 by 9Marks

Published by Crossway
          1300 Crescent Street
          Wheaton, Illinois 60187

Cover image and design: Jordan Singer

First printing 2024

Printed in the United States of America

Trade paperback ISBN: 978-1-4335-9144-0
ePub ISBN: 978-1-4335-9146-4
PDF ISBN: 978-1-4335-9145-7

Library of Congress Cataloging-in-Publication Data

Names: Miller, Daniel P., 1962- author.
Title: What if I've been hurt by my church? / Dan Miller.
Description: Wheaton, Illinois : Crossway, 2024. | Series: Church questions | Includes bibliographical references and index.
Identifiers: LCCN 2023019756 (print) | LCCN 2023019757 (ebook) | ISBN 9781433591440 (trade paperback) | ISBN 9781433591457 (pdf) | ISBN 9781433591464 (epub)
Subjects: LCSH: Clergy—Professional ethics. | Clergy—Sexual behavior. | Sex crimes.
Classification: LCC BV4501.2 .M4729 2024 (print) | LCC BV4501.2 (ebook) | DDC 248.8/92—dc23/eng/20231011
LC record available at https://lccn.loc.gov/2023019756
LC ebook record available at https://lccn.loc.gov/2023019757

Crossway is a publishing ministry of Good News Publishers.

BP		33	32	31	30	29	28	27	26	25	24
15	14	13	12	11	10	9	8	7	6	5	4	3	2	1

Walk in a manner worthy of the calling to which you have been called . . . bearing with one another in love, eager to maintain the unity of the Spirit in the bond of peace.

Ephesians 4:1–3

Healthy churches full of growing saints are breathtaking to behold. God designed churches to protect and build up believers in the faith. And when churches do this job rightly, brothers and sisters spiritually united in Christ can exult in this exquisite gift.

But local churches can also hurt us.

Despite God's glorious purposes, our relationship with the redeemed community can leave us reeling, feeling betrayed, disillusioned, or worse. Maybe you identify with Charles Spurgeon: "The flesh can bear only a certain number of wounds and no more, but the soul can bleed in ten thousand ways, and die over and over again each hour."[1]

In some cases, the source of church pain is interpersonal. A church member offends you with a biting comment or selfish decision. You feel invisible in the church family that once embraced you so warmly. The trust that a ministry leader previously extended to you inexplicably evaporates. A pastor's cool disregard seems reserved for you. Your once-joyful trust in the elders is soured by suspicion.

In other cases, you may feel hurt by some aspect of the church's ministry. A recasting of the church's priorities seems to uproot years of your devoted service to Jesus. A ministry is shuttered against your earnest protestations. The church's financial support of a beloved missionary is terminated. A fruitful gospel partnership ends in bitter dysfunction. Financial struggles become a distasteful emphasis. The church changes course in a way that strikes you as a betrayal of its history, if not a betrayal of Christ. The atmosphere of spiritual zeal that once thrilled your soul in the assembly withers to the point where gathering for worship now proves painful.

Every ministry-engaged member who has walked in fellowship with a local church for any length of time could add a number of examples to these overlapping categories of relational pain.

Amid pain and suffering, we need to remember that we can find hope only in the all-sufficient wisdom of God's revealed word, the ministry of the Holy Spirit, and the edifying support of Christ's church.

At the outset of this book, let me make something clear. Some Christians have suffered inexpressible pain from sexual or spiritual abuse by church leaders who wield their power in godless, soul-crushing ways. This book is *not* designed to speak to those issues. If that describes your situation, I believe you will find edification in this book as you traverse such dark valleys. But this book doesn't directly address your unique suffering.

This book is addressed to church members who are suffering heartache as a consequence of disappointments, sinful choices, and relational offenses. It's also addressed to those who want to help such members.

So the question at hand is both straightforward and difficult: How does God's word counsel us to respond when Christ's body annoys us, frustrates us, or even emotionally wounds us?

The pages that follow respond to that very question. First, we'll learn how to *prepare* for the inevitable disappointment, frustration, and hurt that we'll experience in the local church. Second, we'll consider how to *respond* to hurt when it happens. Finally, we'll consider how to *address our own hearts* in their frustration and hurt.

Preparing for Hurt in the Church

We live in a fallen world. As glorious and wonderful as life in the church is, God's people have not yet been fully delivered from the effects of sin. So we need to learn to set our expectations for life in the church aright. Here are four truths you need to start believing right now to prepare yourself for the inevitable disappointment and hurt you'll inevitably experience in your church.

First, every relationship you have in the church is ultimately about the reputation of Jesus Christ. When I am driven by a Spirit-empowered zeal to exalt Christ as Lord and Savior, I will labor to display his reconciling love in the difficult relationships he ordains for me. Such zeal for Christ's glory must rule my feelings. It must overrule fleshly desires that pull me in other directions. My pain is not all about me. It's ultimately all about Jesus's honor as displayed in the church he died to redeem.

When hurt feelings become more important than Christ's honor in the church, sin is certain to shipwreck our relationships. As Christians, we shouldn't be ruled by our hurt feelings. Instead, we need to cultivate thoughts, words, attitudes, and desires that exalt Jesus. If we allow our feelings, especially hurt feelings, to reign supreme, we will cause damage to his church.

Valuing Christ's glory above our feelings or personal comforts is hard. Our self-oriented culture trains us to put ourselves first, especially when we're in pain. Of course, we shouldn't muzzle our feelings. We must learn to acknowledge and deal with them forthrightly, as we'll consider in a moment. Still, throughout that process, don't ever lose sight of the larger agenda: glorifying Christ and seeing his kingdom exalted. The glory of Jesus displayed in his church must remain our primary ambition amid any pain we endure—even pain in the church.

Second, personal offenses are inevitable in a fallen world. Living in a Genesis 3 world doesn't mean we should dismiss or fatalistically resign ourselves to any offense others may inflict. But it does mean that we—unlike the typical politician, media operative, psychologist, celebrity, or national citizen—believe in human depravity. We should therefore anticipate the ways depravity will make our lives difficult.

People will sinfully offend you. Your feelings will get ruffled if not pierced through by the words, decisions, and deeds of others. When this happens, don't be shocked. Nothing strange is happening. Don't buy the lie that your hurt is somehow unique. It's not (1 Cor. 10:13).

You don't plan a summer picnic with friends and then fall into deep depression if the gathering is rained out. You knew it could happen. It's a bummer, but you adjust your plans. Similarly, we shouldn't despair when sinners sin. We shouldn't despair when weak people prove inadequate in ways that negatively affect us. Suffering pain due to the failures of others is a given in our fallen world. We should never react to the sins of others as if we missed this memo.

Realizing the inevitability of hurt feelings in a cursed world doesn't solve that hurt, of course. But it might soften the blow just a bit. It might adjust your expectations and help deliver you from the downward spiral of outrage or shock that someone dared hurt your feelings. The world will not end. You will suffer offense again. But God's grace will help you journey forward in a manner that proves Jesus is indeed your Savior and soul's ultimate delight. Wherever and whenever you encounter sin in your community, know that there and then grace abounds.

Third, suffering offense presents a God-ordained opportunity to mature in Christ. Stop and ask yourself, What might be God's purpose in your suffering, according to Scripture? God has a plan for our suffering—he's sovereign over it. Surely, Jesus didn't ordain suffering in your life to give you the opportunity to vent your outrage, retaliate, gossip, spiral into depression, or withdraw from others in self-pitying resignation and wounded pride.

Instead, God promises in the Bible that everything he ordains for you—even suffering—serves to mature your faith for his glory and for your ultimate joy (Rom. 5:3–5; 8:28–29; Heb. 12:7–11; James 1:2–4). This promise applies not only to times of general misfortune but equally to occasions when you suffer offense.

Fourth, human emotions are easily twisted by sin. Emotions are not evil. They are good gifts from God. The Creator, whose image we bear, displays a wide array of holy emotions (Gen. 6:5–6; Num. 11:1; Ps. 2:4; Hos. 11:7–9; Zeph. 3:17; John 11:35) and calls us to do likewise (Josh. 1:9; Ps. 100:1; Isa. 22:12; Eph. 4:26; Phil. 4:4).

At the same time, our emotions have been corrupted by sin. They can sabotage us, compromising our fellowship with God and his people.

Our emotional lives are complicated. Even well-meaning Christians disagree on how to think best about and counsel negative emotions. But for our purposes, let's just focus on the fundamentals. Scripture stresses our moral responsibility for our emotional responses (Lev. 19:17–18; Pss. 32:11; 37:4; 106:32–33 with Deut. 32:48–52; Matt. 5:22; Eph. 4:26, 31). However innocently feelings of relational hurt may arise in our hearts, we are morally responsible for how we respond to and display that pain. If we're honest with ourselves, we know that often our immediate reactions to offense are rooted in sinful desires lurking in the dark recesses of our hearts.

By way of qualification, acknowledging that sin corrupts our emotions doesn't dismiss or delimit the genuine suffering that a believer may experience. Feeling hurt isn't wrong. What matters is how we respond to those feelings. Being hurt by others doesn't exempt us from moral accountability. Even in the gloom, there is always a visible path leading to righteousness.

By implication, it's never wise to grant diplomatic immunity to any of our emotional responses to relational hurt. We may lack the power to control every aspect of every emotional reaction that other people's words or actions ignite in us. But we are responsible for rightly responding to those reactions and repenting whenever they prove sinful.

These four foundations—the priority of Christ's glory, the inevitability of relational turmoil, God's promise to edify us through trials, and our moral responsibility to steward our emotions—provide the convictions we need to respond rightly to offenses we suffer in our churches.

Responding Biblically to Feelings of Hurt and Frustration

Now that we've got the foundations in place, let's talk about how to respond to personal offenses in the church.

First, learn to delay judgment. Wounded feelings love to bolt from the gate like a racehorse; we are tempted to move from feelings to judgment in a moment's notice. Thankfully, Scripture counsels us to delay judgment in the interest of a more thorough, levelheaded investigation. Proverbs 18:13 teaches, "If one gives an answer before he hears, / it is his folly and shame."

Hurt feelings cloud our perception, tempting us to invent details, confuse facts, misremember statements, and stuff self-serving conclusions into the gaps in our knowledge. We all know from experience just how easy it is to supply unreasonable, emotionally charged explanations for why our offender chose to hurt us in a particular way.

But suffering wrong never cancels our need to decelerate judgment. The perception that someone has sinned against me does not give me the sovereign authority to determine reality with respect to myself or my offender. We must let the passing of time unearth facts that may illuminate a more accurate understanding of events. We always want to live according to the truth because truth matters to God. So if hasty judgments and raw emotions crowd out the genuine pursuit of truth, then we need to recognize that our emotions are not helping us. We need to learn to tap the brakes on quick judgments when we are wronged.

Second, consciously entrust yourself to God in prayer. When Jesus suffered unjustly, "he did not threaten, but continued entrusting himself to him who judges justly" (1 Pet. 2:23). When we suffer an offense or hurt, we easily rely on fleshly wisdom and fixate on self-reliant counterresponses. But instead, we need to prayerfully place such matters in God's keeping. We must practice walking by faith, laying down our fleshly weapons, and turning the offense over in prayer to the jurisdiction of our heavenly advocate.

Remind yourself, "This is God's fight more than it is mine." Doing so is liberating. His honor, not ours, is at stake. And believe me, he can handle things! As Isaac Watts reminded us, "He sits on no precarious throne."[2]

Third, thoughtfully assess the desires of your heart. Examining your own heart amid hurt is challenging. We can feel so unstable on the inside that the last thing we want to do is take a long look at our hearts. And, of course, you may need to let the dust settle a bit. But spiritual maturity shortens the delay between the initial feelings of woundedness and the first moment of clearheaded self-analysis. Learn to ask these hard questions as early as possible: "What do I most want in this matter? Are my feelings of discontent connected to an unmet desire or a thwarted ambition?"

Questions like these reveal that much of our hurt comes from wounded pride, selfish desire, idolatrously held personal opinions, stubborn refusal to receive correction, an insistence on "being me," and similar deformities that live in our hearts (see James 4:1–3).

I've come to believe that the majority of offenses I have personally suffered in the context of my church would never have occurred apart from sin residing in me. I have also profited by resolving those offenses in the quiet of my soul by identifying and confessing the inordinate and self-serving desires that fueled my offense. Do this. I'm confident you will experience similar benefits.

Fourth, pursue reconciliation with your offender. Sometimes we should practice "overlook[ing] an offense" without saying anything to our offenders (Prov. 19:11; cf. Eph. 4:2; Col. 3:13). This may be the case when the offense is more accidental than intentional or more isolated rather than character- istic. You know that a forgiving spirit turns your heart toward that person, and you can cheerfully move on.

Yet sometimes we should also speak to the offender because our hearts continue to strug- gle, because we are genuinely concerned about their spiritual condition, or because we know that our relationship needs repair. In these cases, humbly approach your offender not with the goal of venting, getting something off your chest so that you might feel better, or making the person feel bad. If that's the motivation of your heart, hold back. Take time to pray until you can approach the person in love.

Then—take two—approach your offender with the goal of repairing your relationship.

Believe it or not, Jesus assigned the offended party the responsibility to initiate a conversation with the offender in the interest of peace: "If your brother sins against you, go and tell him his fault" (Matt. 18:15; cf. Luke 17:3–4). The apostle Paul's counsel, "If possible, so far as it depends on you, live peaceably with all" (Rom. 12:18), requires not only passive but also active obedience—intentional, proactive peacemaking.

The one option that Jesus does not make available to us is the "in-between" option—something in between cheerfully forbearing and moving on and discussing the offense with our offender. The trouble is, the "in-between" option is easiest and most gratifying to the flesh. We naturally respond to offense by silently stewing in our own sadness. Or by tearing down our offender before others—venting our anger to people who have no right to know about and no capacity to repair our relational rift. We naturally fume, grow bitter, gossip, wallow in self-pity, withdraw, or turn a cold shoulder.

It's also common to wait for our offender to apologize. "He hurt me," we reason, "so it's his job to talk to me. I'm the one hurting here!" Or, "If she doesn't recognize that she has offended me, that's all the proof I need that she does not truly love me!" Such relational positioning is poison to the soul; it fractures the unity of the church. It's the polar opposite of being "eager to maintain the unity of the spirit in the bond of peace" that is our high calling as members of Christ's body (Eph. 4:3).

Jesus perceived the folly of demanding that others read your mind and share your exact feelings. He also torpedoed the silent-suffering approach, which is why, again, he said, "If your brother sins against you, go . . ." Having honest and loving conversations is not an approach our world typically encourages. But we are not followers of the world (1 John 2:15–17).

Striving for reconciliation with others demands that I love Jesus and his church more than I love nursing my sense of offense. Such love for Jesus flows from a Spirit-supplied appreciation that the Lord chose to pursue me, not withdraw; to engage me, not pout; to redeem me, not reject me (Rom. 3:9–18; 5:8–

11). Zeal for Christ inspires us to follow in his steps, not hone the craft of erecting relational barriers.

Fifth, pursue forgiveness. The ultimate aim of approaching your offender is forgiveness and reconciliation. Mustering the courage to speak to a fellow church member may prove extremely difficult. Forgiveness may prove harder still.

But the gospel gives us the power to forgive others because we, as followers of Christ, recognize that we are sinners who have received God's forgiveness ourselves. We are experienced recipients of his reconciling grace—so we have an advantage that unbelievers do not possess. The gospel supplies us with a powerful motivation to forgive those who sin against us (Matt. 18:23–35).

The gospel also satisfies our demand for justice. First, we know that Christ died to pay the full cost of every sin any of our brothers or sisters could ever commit against us (Rom. 4:4–8; 8:1; Col. 2:13–14). Second, we know that on the final day, the Judge of all flesh will render perfect judgment (Ps. 9:7–8; 1 Cor. 4:1–5; 2 Cor. 5:10). We can possess full certainty that no one is ever getting away with anything! Not only may we rest in these tandem truths but we must determine to operate in faith according to them as we relate to other sinners.

We must also think clearly about the communal aspects of biblical forgiveness. Forgiveness isn't a unilateral process calibrated to free our spirit of the noxious emotions of unforgiveness. The ultimate aim of forgiveness is not us feeling better; it's reconciliation—and reconciliation is an innately relational enterprise. So forgiveness isn't an individual quest for relief. It's a quest for relational restoration that is, to a significant degree, concerned with the unity of Christ's body. Accordingly, this pursuit will often benefit from, if not require, godly counsel as faithful brothers and sisters in Christ come alongside to help us navigate the reconciliation process.

Responding to hurt in these ways will not erase your suffering. Praise God if one or two of these skills dislodged sin in your heart from which you have now repented. But for many, the pain will persist. Indeed, applying some of these truths may increase your pain. So where do we go from here? Let's consider five ways to respond redemptively to the relational hurt we might experience in the church.

Addressing Our Hearts amid Church Hurt

First, face your hurt and describe it as accurately as possible. A nameless terror is doubly terrorizing. The psalmists of Israel did not ignore their suffering, minimize it, run from it, or pride themselves in toughing it out. They faced and expressed their pain.[3]

And they got specific.

They did not speak in general terms of gargantuan ghosts lurking about in murky shadows. They suffered specific wrongs and named those wrongs. In Psalm 69:4, for instance, David writes that his enemies hated him without cause and attacked him with lies. A nameless, faceless heartache has the power to become a boogeyman bigger than anything that could actually fit under your bed. Naming the wrong done to you helps whittle the hurt down to size (cf. Pss. 142:1–4; 143:3–4).

Being specific about our suffering hedges our sorrows and keeps them from taking on all-powerful, all-present status in our minds. It also helps us plug our little stories into God's grand redemptive narrative and thus keep everything in proper perspective.

Second, wait patiently and expectantly for relief. Only God endures forever. Your hurt has no such lasting power. We cannot determine or manipulate an end to our suffering. Yet we may rejoice that no trial will ever outlive God's grace. In Psalm 40:1–2, King David writes,

> I waited patiently for the LORD;
>> he inclined to me and heard my cry.
> He drew me up from the pit of
>> destruction,
>> out of the miry bog,
> and set my feet upon a rock,
>> making my steps secure.

David "waited patiently." This waiting is an "active" waiting. In other words, David isn't talking about the kind of waiting one does while scrolling aimlessly on a smartphone at an airport terminal. David is talking about enduring suffering while anticipating relief—like an archer struggling to hold a taut bowstring, awaiting the captain's command to release the arrow. We want every hurt to disappear immediately. We must instead learn the discipline of active waiting, even if it turns out we must wait until we meet Jesus.

Third, stop listening to yourself and start talking to yourself. Twentieth-century Welsh preacher Martyn Lloyd-Jones famously said, "Have you realized that most of your unhappiness in life is due to the fact that you are listening to yourself instead of talking to yourself?" He continued, "The main art in the matter of spiritual living is to know how to handle yourself. You have to take yourself in hand, you have to address yourself, preach to yourself, question yourself."[4]

That's sound advice. If you're hurting, choose to meditate on the truth God has revealed in his written word and preach that truth to your soul. The psalmists often "took themselves in hand" this way:

Why are you cast down, O my soul . . . ? (Ps. 42:5; 43:5)

For God alone, O my soul, wait in silence. (Ps. 62:5)

Bless the LORD, O my soul. (Ps. 103:2; 104:1)

Return, O my soul, to your rest. (Ps. 116:7)

When we suffer hurt, our emotions start telling us self-coddling messages that lure us into playing the "if only" movie on the big screen of our mind. "If only I had said this. If only she had not said that. If only the elders were wiser men. If only more members had seen the light and objected. If only I had skipped that event." Whether or not it's self-pity, agonizing over the way things should have gone, or one of a thousand similar mindsets, letting your wounded heart sing any solo it chooses is unwise.

Instead, learn to preach to yourself.

Again, we find this practice throughout the Psalms. The psalmists honestly voice their hurts and lament their suffering, but they typically followed those cries of anguish with a response of hope—a "but God."

This shift in focus might recall God's redemptive works in salvation history (Pss. 22:1–5; 77:10–15; 85:1–7), one of his attributes (Pss. 115:1–11; 116:1–7), or one of his promises (Ps. 119:50–51). Nothing substitutes for the voice of God echoing in the chamber of your soul.

English Puritan William Gouge (1575–1653) once beautifully exemplified how to preach the gospel to yourself amid suffering. Reflecting on the deepest trials of his life, he reminded himself that his suffering could not separate him from the love of God. "In all these [sufferings]," he wrote, "there is nothing of hell, or of God's wrath."[5] Gouge's biographer observed that Gouge believed his sufferings were never so deep that he could not see the bottom of them and say, "Soul, be silent: soul, be patient. It is thy God and Father who thus ordereth thy condition. Thou art his clay, and he may tread and trample on thee as He pleaseth. Thou hast deserved much more. It is enough that thou art kept out of hell."[6]

Such also are the reasoned convictions of a soul that has grown skillful in applying the salve of the gospel to hurts suffered in a broken world. Wounded feelings can't steer us toward gospel hope. But meditating on God's revealed word does just that.

Fourth, keep praying, even when it seems God is not listening—no, especially when it seems God is not listening. As an old preacher once said, "Resolve never to be dumb while God is deaf."[7]

Scripture unmistakably teaches that God rules sovereignly over all that comes to pass, including evil (Gen. 15:12–16; 50:15, 18–20; Judg. 14:1–4; 1 Kings 22:1–23; Job 1:1–2:10; Eph. 1:11). Confidence in that truth and in the fact that God listens to the prayers of his people consoled the psalmists in their suffering and shaped their prayers.

Facing internal travail and external attack, King David cried, "How long, O LORD? Will you forget me forever?" (Ps. 13:1). David's prayers went unanswered. He felt forgotten, abandoned by the Lord. *Yet he kept praying.* Amazingly, David closes the psalm by singing and rejoicing that the Lord "has dealt bountifully with me" (Ps. 13:6).

David does not detail his transition from feeling harassed and abandoned to his state of triumphant praise. It may have taken a long time. Indeed, breaking free from a season in which we feel abandoned by God on account of our suffering may seem interminably long. But like David in Psalm 13, we will once again see the brightness of the Lord's face. Until then, may he find us praying, trusting, and sheltering securely under his protective wings.

Fifth, look long and longingly for glory. Keep your hope fixed on the final day. Meditating on the return of Christ won't eliminate the suffering you must endure now, but it will keep it in perspective. A day is coming when sin and Satan will be history. On that day, Jesus will render final judgment and reward based on his holy, infallible standard (1 Cor. 4:3–5; 2 Cor. 5:10). Act today in anticipation of that final accounting before the throne of the universe.

Maybe write these words down somewhere, or post them on your bathroom mirror: "Suffering, then glory." That's the pattern of the Christian life. It's how Jesus lived, and what he promised for his followers. So don't be surprised by the suffering, but keep your eyes fixed on the glory. Didn't Jesus do exactly this? "Who for the joy that was set before him endured the cross" (Heb. 12:2).

A Final Word on the Sanctifying Power of Disillusionment

Having read to this point, you may find yourself saying, "Yes, okay, but my heart still aches. I'm devastated, and nothing will change that. The sorrow I've experienced in relation to my local church hurts so deeply that I feel hopeless."

The church is the place we run to for refuge, yet it can become a place of frustration and pain.

That pain is real, and it's deep. But consider that it may be a gift from God designed to draw you closer to himself.

As surely as Jesus cleared the temple courts with a whip, he will just as faithfully smash the idols of your heart. Jesus can use the disillusionment we suffer in the context of a local church to topple idols of comfort, ease, relational depth, or affirmation we have erected in our hearts. It is not always easy to discern, let alone to admit, when Jesus is using the pain of disillusionment to root out idolatrous interests and fleshly desires. But whenever our local church becomes a source of pain, we should carefully consider this possibility.

One of the most profound books to reflect on that topic is Dietrich Bonhoeffer's classic work *Life Together*. Bonhoeffer exhorts us to recognize the *benefits* of growing disillusioned with a faith community, as odd as that may seem. I know "benefits" may be a hard word to read in that context, but his reasoning is solid.[8]

When a local church becomes a source of hurt, we naturally grow disillusioned. Since disillusionment is painful, we easily regard the church as an enemy. But wisely managed, disillusionment can serve as a beneficial misery— a torment that purifies the soul. Simply put, disillusionment liberates us from illusion. It's a pin that pops the balloon of lies we've chosen to believe.

In our fallen state we sometimes wrongly operate from illusions, misconceptions, and things we imagine to be true. But living according to an illusion is not just false but can be dangerous. The young son of a gangster may benefit temporarily from the illusion that his father is a brave, hardworking man. But if his illusions aren't eventually crushed, he may well follow his father into a life of crime. Illusions that persist too long damage the soul.

We're prone to embrace illusions in the early stages of any important relationship. A newly married couple entertains illusions about marriage and about one another: "My spouse will never hurt me. Now I can live happily ever after." Prospective members form illusions about their new church: "The pastors here would never make a decision I'd disagree with." "The community here is so loving. It would never let me down." "The preaching here is so biblical. I'll never be disappointed by another sermon." But these illusions are eventually overwhelmed by reality. The illusion of an ideal church, much like the illusion of a perfect marriage, eventually bursts.

When it does, we often point the finger at those we think caused our disillusionment. We respond with frustration or anger; we might even find it difficult to go on liking them. But we need to resist the temptation to turn our disappointments into opportunities for sin. We should be particularly on guard against retaliatory anger, social withdrawal, bitterness, a cynical or superior spirit, and unyielding despair. Instead, we must learn to value the pain of disillusionment as a purifying valley we must pass through in order to reap the spiritual rewards that await us on the other side.

Genuine love, love based on truth and not illusions, looks at all the disappointing sinners in our church and says, "You are a gift from God just as you are. And I love you as you are, not as you exist in my dreams." As Bonhoeffer notes, if we have biblical expectations, if we live according to the truth, we'll be able to enter the church "not as demanders, but as thankful recipients."[9]

When we love our dream of what a church community should be more than what that community actually is, we idolize a fantasy and reject an *actual* gift of God. Letting go of our illusions can lead us to the verdant fields of genuine love for one another—the kind of hard-won love produced by perseverance. It also leads to a sweeter communion with the Master who promises to bless those who mourn (Matt. 5:4).

We live in a broken world, and that brokenness passes right through our local churches. It also passes right through our fallen hearts. But as Christians, we believe a full restoration is coming (Rom. 8:18–30). When it does, our faith will become sight, and all our suffering will be gone forever.

Until then, God calls us to a path of endurance for his glory—endurance that includes painful church relationships. That call may sound daunting, but our Savior promises never to leave us or forsake us (John 10:7–30; Heb. 13:5). Knowing that Jesus is with us all the way to the end makes all the difference—today, tomorrow, and forever.

Recommended Resources

Dietrich Bonhoeffer, *Life Together*, trans. John W. Doberstein (New York: HarperCollins, 1978).

C. S. Lewis, *The Problem of Pain* (1940; repr., New York: HarperCollins, 1996).

Notes

1. Charles Spurgeon, *The Treasury of David*, 2 vols. (1869; repr., Nashville: Thomas Nelson, 1984) 2:3.
2. Isaac Watts, "Keep Silence, All Created Things" (1890), Hymnary.org, https://hymnary.org/.
3. In this section I often draw from the fuller consideration of this topic in Walter C. Kaiser Jr., *A Biblical Approach to Personal Suffering* (Chicago: Moody Press, 1982).
4. Martin Lloyd-Jones, *Spiritual Depression: Its Causes and Cure* (Grand Rapids, MI: Eerdmans, 1965), 20–21.
5. Mark Dever, *The Message of the Old Testament: Promises Made* (Wheaton, IL: Crossway, 2006), 618. Dever cites James Reid, *Memoirs of the Westminster Divines*, 2 vols. (Paisley, UK: Stephen and Andrew Young, 1815), 1:358.
6. Reid, *Memoirs of the Westminster Divines*, 1:358, cited in Dever, *Message of the Old Testament*, 618.
7. George Swinnock, quoted in Charles Spurgeon, *Treasury of David*, 1:156.

8. Dietrich Bonhoeffer, *Life Together*, trans. John W. Doberstein (New York: Harper and Row, 1954), 26–30, 93.
9. Bonhoeffer, *Life Together*, 28

Scripture Index

IX 9Marks

Building Healthy Churches

9Marks exists to equip church leaders with a biblical vision and practical resources for displaying God's glory to the nations through healthy churches.

To that end, we want to see churches characterized by these nine marks of health:

1. Expositional Preaching
2. Gospel Doctrine
3. A Biblical Understanding of Conversion and Evangelism
4. Biblical Church Membership
5. Biblical Church Discipline
6. A Biblical Concern for Discipleship and Growth
7. Biblical Church Leadership
8. A Biblical Understanding of the Practice of Prayer
9. A Biblical Understanding and Practice of Missions

Find all our Crossway titles and other resources at 9Marks.org.

John Onwuchekwa · Church Questions

Sam Emadi · Church Questions

Mark Dever · Church Questions

...el Like ...o Church?

IX 9Marks
What
Is a
Church?
Matthew
Emadi · Church Questions

IX 9Marks
How Do I Get
Started in
Evangelism?
Mack
Stiles · Church Questions

IX 9Marks
How Can
Women T...
the Local...
Keri
Folmar · Church Questions

...zed?

IX 9Marks
Who's in
Charge of
the Church?
Sam
Emadi · Church Questions

IX 9Marks
How Can
I Serve My
Church?
Matthew
Emadi · Church Questions

IX 9Marks
How Can
I Love Ch...
Members
Different...
Jonathan
& Andy N...· Church Questions

IX 9Marks Church Questions

Providing ordinary Christians with sound and
accessible biblical teaching by answering
common questions about church life.

For more information, visit crossway.org.